The Complete Guide to

Manifestation With 369

Number Wisdom for Creating Your Own Destiny

ANDREW COOK

Don't forget to purchase the companion journal,

The Complete Guide to Manifestation With 369 Journal

This 120-page guided journal allows you to directly apply the numerology concepts from the book through thoughtful prompts, exercises, and space to record your unique 369 observations and manifestations. By actively journaling your insights, you will gain clarity, strengthen intuitive abilities, and witness the power of 369 unfold in your daily life. The journal's inspiring design and high-vibration activations will help you integrate the magic of 369 angel numbers into your spiritual path on a whole new level. Take your manifestation abilities to the next level by grabbing your copy of The Complete Guide to Manifestation With 369 Journal today!

CONTENTS

INTRODUCTION

Have you ever noticed the numbers 3, 6, and 9 popping up around you on a regular basis? Perhaps you've glanced at a clock and it's 3:39, received $369 in unexpected money, or awakened feeling deeply renewed multiple times per week. What if I told you that seeing these numbers repeatedly is much more than mere coincidence?

The recurring appearance of the 369 sequences in your life is divinely guided. These numbers are subtle messages and affirmations from the Universe, confirming that you are on the right path and urging you to keep going. When you notice 369, it is a sign of alignment. It is a sign that you are tuned in to higher frequencies of manifestation and that your desires, hopes, and dreams are on their way to you right now!

In this book, I will show you just how powerful the 369 sequence is for supercharging your manifestation abilities. Seeing 369, especially in clusters and repeated patterns, puts you in perfect energetic alignment with the Law of Attraction and unlocks a stream of guidance, synchronicity, and good fortune.

The messages from the Universe are always loving, but sometimes they can be subtle. Most people miss or dismiss the appearance of 369 and other number sequences in their lives as random coincidences. But the truth is that these numbers are imbued with divine guidance and meaning. They serve as a form of communication between the spiritual realm and the physical realm. The more attention you pay to them, the more they will appear as affirmations, validation, and instructions for manifesting your desires.

My journey with the 369 sequences began during a period of financial struggle in my life. I was stressed, overworked, and constantly worried about money no matter how hard I worked. One day, I noticed the numbers 369 appear over and over everywhere around me - on receipts, license plates, addresses, and most notably, on clocks anytime I just happened to glance at them. I started researching the meaning behind this sequence and realized it was a message for me. It was the Universe urging me to shift into a mindset of abundance, have faith in receiving provision, and claim my desires.

I decided to start incorporating 369 into my daily life. I would do affirmations, vision boards, and meditations focused on the numbers. I even used the 369 sequences as a mantra, repeating it aloud and in my mind. What transpired next amazed me. Within just a few weeks, I started experiencing financial "miracles". Checks for hundreds or thousands of dollars would show up in my mailbox unexpectedly. I would get random Venmo payments from old friends I hadn't spoken to in years. My business would explode with new clients I never even advertised to. This was all divinely guided 369 manifestations in action!

The more I paid attention to the 369 signs around me

and used the numbers intentionally, the more miracles, big and small, I experienced in all areas of my life - not just money. Seeing 369 became my signal from the Universe that I was on the right path and that magic was on its way.

We all can use 369 manifestations to remove blocks and resistance, align with divine guidance, and realize our wildest dreams. But first, we must open our awareness to receive the messages. That is why I have created this book - to open your eyes to the power of 369 that is already surrounding you every day!

In these pages, I will show you step-by-step how to harness the magical energy of 369 manifestation. You'll learn how to interpret the deeper meaning when 369 appears for you as well as actionable techniques for using 369 energies to manifest like never before.

Here's just a tiny sample of what we'll cover:

o Specific 369 sequences to watch for and what they mean (like 3:39 on clocks or seeing $369 repeatedly)

o Powerful 369 affirmations, visualizations, meditations, and journaling prompts

o Real-life success stories and examples of 369 manifestation magic

o How to use 369 energies to remove mental and energetic blocks

o Combining 369 with other powerful numbers like 222, 444, and more

o Troubleshooting tips for when you don't see 369

or results seem slow.

The Universe speaks to every single one of us through signs, symbols, and synchronicity. But it's up to us to open our awareness, to receive guidance and act on it. Manifesting with 369 is one of the most effortless and exciting ways to do this! The more you pay attention to 369 energies, the more it will show up and confirm you are aligned with your desires.

If you are ready to stop waiting and wishing for what you want and finally take action to manifest the life of your dreams, this book will guide the way! I can't wait for you to experience the abundance, fulfillment, and joy that come from working with 369 energies. No matter what area of life you are looking to improve - finances, relationships, health, career - 369 is the key.

The Universe has already sent you millions of 369 sequences. They have been urging you to wake up and start consciously manifesting! So, let's get started. Turn the page, open your awareness, and get ready to manifest like you never have before. Abundance, happiness, and success are waiting for you!

CHAPTER 1
UNDERSTANDING NUMBER
SEQUENCES AND MANIFESTATION

Do you ever feel like the Universe is trying to send you hints, clues or messages? Have you ever noticed the same numbers or number patterns appearing repeatedly in your life? If so, congratulations - the Universe is indeed communicating directly with you!

These seemingly coincidental numbers you notice have profound spiritual meanings and insight to offer. They are subtle "winks" from the divine, confirming you are on the right path and urging you to keep following the signs. When you start paying closer attention to these number sequences, a whole world of guidance, synchronicity, and magic opens to you.

In this chapter, we'll dive deep into numerology - the study of the mystical meanings of numbers. We'll explore how numbers carry energy and how being aware of number patterns can support your spiritual growth and manifestation abilities. Most importantly, we'll introduce the profound power of the 369 sequences. Seeing 369, especially repeatedly, is one of the clearest signs you can receive from the Universe. It is a sign you are aligned with your desires, and they are coming to fruition.

Decode the Messages Within Every Number

Numerology teaches us that all numbers carry their own unique energetic vibration and significance. Just like colors, symbols, animals, and tarot cards contain hidden meanings, every number represents spiritual qualities and influences as well.

Numbers are the language of the Universe. Though we live in a physical world, there are subtle energetic frequencies that always impact and guide us. Being aware of the energetic meaning within numbers allows us to tune into divine guidance from the Universe and spiritual realm more easily.

Specific numbers also unlock different manifestations powers. Each number has its own set of meanings and influences our reality in different ways when we focus on it intentionally.

Here are just a few examples of the energetic meanings and manifestation powers of common numbers:

- New beginnings, fresh starts, optimism, confidence

- Balance, harmony, partnerships, cooperation

- Self-expression, creativity, optimism, joy

- Grounding, stability, focus, determination

- Change, adventure, freedom, versatility

o   Harmony, family, domesticity, balance

o   Spirituality, wisdom, intuition, inner knowing

o   Wealth, success, abundance, authority

o   Completion, humanitarianism, benevolence

As you can see, all numbers have their own essence and Areas of influence. When a particular number stands out to you or appears in patterns, it brings the energy and meanings of that number into your awareness. Paying attention to which numbers are showing up for you the most can provide powerful guidance on your life path and desires.

For example, are you noticing the number 7 frequently as you embark on a new spiritual journey? This is confirmation you are following your intuition and inner wisdom. Or perhaps 4's and 8's will pop up as you build your new business. This signals success, prosperity and strong foundations are manifesting!

Numbers also combine their energies when appearing in sequences. So, while 1 represents new beginnings, the number 111 amplifies and strengthens this meaning. When you notice interplaying numbers like 111, 333, 444 etc. it means that a number's themes and energies are powerfully present for you.

Of all the number sequences, none are more powerful than 369. This potent trio amplifies themes of optimism, inspiration, creativity, and manifestation. 3, 6 and 9 are already highly spiritual numbers on their own, and their powers expand exponentially when combined. Seeing 369 is one of the clearest signs you can receive from the

Universe about impending manifestations.

Messages From Your Angels: Angel Numbers

Many numerologists believe numbers that stand out or appear in noticeable patterns are messages sent from your guardian angels and spirit guides. These notable number sequences are known as Angel Numbers.

Seeing specific Angel Numbers is a sign your angels are by your side, validating you and offering encouragement, advice, or confirmation about your path. Angel Numbers also serve as little reminders to keep your thoughts positive and aligned with your desires.

Your angels want to support you on your life journey, but they can't interfere or directly intervene most of the time. So, they use subtle signs like repeating numbers to send you guidance and inspiration from the spiritual realm.

Here are some examples of common Angel Numbers and what they may signify:

111 - New opportunities, trust your path

222 - Have faith, relationships need balance

333 - Ascended masters are near, amplify creativity

444 - Angels surround you, invite more peace

555 - Positive changes are ahead, embrace them

666 - Focus thoughts on love, not fear

777 - You are on the right path, keep going

888 - Financial abundance is manifesting

999 - Completion of a life chapter, prepare for new

1111 - Make positive affirmations, new intentions

1212 - Divine timing, everything is perfectly unfolding

When you notice any of these Angel Numbers showing up for you in noticeable and repetitive patterns, consider it a loving sign from angels. This is their way of affirming that you are supported, guided, and aligning with your highest path. Stay centered in faith and gratitude when these numbers appear.

Your angels also want to reassure you that the end of struggle is near - solutions, rewards and manifestations are unfolding. Keep following the signs! Angel Numbers are heavenly timestamps confirming you are on the brink of a breakthrough.

Understanding 369 Energy

Now that we've covered how numbers carry meaning and how sequences deliver messages from angels, let's focus specifically on the power of 369. This potent trio is one of the most divine combinations of numbers you can receive guidance from. Seeing 369, especially repeatedly, puts you in perfect energetic alignment to manifest your desires through optimism and inner power.

Let's break down the unique attributes of 3, 6 and 9 and how they add up to a vibration of manifestation magic:

3 - Represents optimism, joy, creativity, imagination. Channels Divine mind and intuition.

6 - Represents harmony, balance, nurturing family. Heals energy blocks and shadows.

9 - Represents global consciousness, humanitarianism, benevolence. Embodies unconditional love and light working.

When 3, 6 and 9 appear together, their attributes combine to amplify each other. This creates an energy surge of creative inspiration, self-empowerment, healing alignment and unconditional love. You are catapulted into the optimal headspace and vibration for manifesting your dreams!

369 also contains hints of Yin and Yang energy - the perfect balance of the divine feminine and masculine. The 3 and 9 contain more divine feminine qualities of intuition and compassion. While the 6 holds the divine masculine qualities of strength, provision, and protection.

Seeing 369 is a sign you are balanced, aligned and ready to take inspired action. You are fully supported from above, so march forward boldly knowing all of creation is working on your behalf!

In addition, when you add up 3 + 6 + 9, they total 18. Break that down further and you get 9. The number 9 represents completion, achievements and living at your highest self. It is no coincidence that 369 energetically compounds into the number of completion and manifestation.

This numerical makeup confirms that 369 carries enormous potential to complete life chapters and hurriedly manifest your desires. Keep seeing 369? Then you are right on the brink of major breakthroughs!

Tuning Into 369 Energy

Your angels and spirit team broadcast 369 sequences into your awareness when you are most in need of them. They will appear more frequently during times of confusion, stagnation, or doubt. Consider 369 a heavenly "traffic signal" urging you to keep going and trusting your path.

Here are some of the common ways 369 may show up to catch your attention:

o   Glancing at the clock right at 3:39, 13:33, etc.

o   Receiving $369 back as change at the store.

o   369 appear in phone numbers, addresses, license plates.

o   Finding 369 in mathematical equations or adding up totals

o   A song with 369 lyrics plays on shuffle during contemplation.

o   You wake up naturally at 3:33am or 6:39am repeatedly.

o   "Likes" or views on social media landing at 369 or increments.

o   Seeing clusters like 369369 or 963963 in sequences

o   Intuitively "feeling" prompted to look up and notice 369 around you.

Stay alert for both subtle and prominent appearances of 369 in your daily life. When you witness these signals, immediately take it as confirmation you are headed down the right path. Let 369 boost your mood, energize your manifestations, and assure you of impending breakthroughs.

You may be wondering why you notice some numbers like 369 more than other sequences. Your soul resonates at a unique vibrational frequency, as do all numbers. You are naturally more inclined to notice numbers containing your soul's special energy essence. So, if you witness 369 often, it is likely those numbers match your soul's energy perfectly.

You may also have a special connection with the Ascended Master and Archangel energies associated with 3, 6 and 9. These include:

Archangel Gabriel (Guidance & Enlightenment)

Archangel Metatron (Divine Alchemy)

Ascended Master Kuthumi (Wisdom & Truth)

Seeing their numbers is a sign they are near and supporting you on your spiritual path.

Once you become familiar with the meanings of 369 energy, you gain spiritual currency with the Universe. Moving forward, you can translate every 369 appearances as a personalized message just for you. Here are some examples:

o   Seeing 369 after making an important decision is confirmation you made the right choice.

- o Seeing 369 during financial turmoil means abundance is manifesting soon.

- o Seeing 369 after meeting your soulmate confirms they are the "real deal".

- o Seeing 369 after applying for a dream job signals you will get it.

- o Seeing 369 while envisioning your goals means they are crystallizing.

The Universe continually sends you signs through 369 energies. But it's up to you to tune in, interpret the guidance and take inspired action. Use 369 as your special cheer squad, perpetually reminding you to believe in yourself and your manifestation abilities.

Harnessing 369 Energy to Manifest Faster

Now that you understand the deeper meaning of 369 sequences, let's discuss ways to intentionally harness 369 energies to manifest your desires faster. Seeing 369 is one thing, but learning to integrate it into your spiritual practices is game changing.

Here are some suggested techniques for leveraging 369 energies:

369 Manifestation Meditations:

Close your eyes and sit quietly. Visualize the numbers 369 illuminating before you. Imagine their energy radiating a glowing white light. Let this light infuse into your body and aura. Feel yourself absorbing the high-vibrational energy of creativity, inspiration, love, and abundance. How does your body feel sitting in this amplified 369 energy?

Notice any blockages dissipating. Hold space here meditating in the 369 vibrations for as long as desired.

369 Manifestation Affirmations:

Choose a desire you want to manifest. Write down an affirmation statement incorporating 369 such as: "I am attracting my dream job with ease, optimism and wisdom (369 energy)." Repeat this statement aloud or silently throughout your day with intention. Harness the manifesting power of your words and the 369 vibrations.

369 Manifestation Journaling:

Journaling is a powerful manifestation tool combining writing and introspection. Each day, write down all the places you witnessed 369 sequences. Track any insights, aha moments or growth that occurred after seeing 369. Record how 369 makes you feel and any desires you want to focus this energy on manifesting.

369 Vision Boards:

Vision boards allow you to tangibly visualize your dreams as already manifested. Cut out pictures, words, quotes representing your desires. Intentionally decorate your board with 369 sequences using numbers, patterns, or writing it out. Gaze at your finished 369 board often to crystallize these dreams into reality.

There are so many other ways to infuse 369 energy into your spiritual practices like Tarot readings, crystals grids, prayers, mantras and more. Get creative and let this numerical sequence guide you to greater alignment and manifestation power.

Troubleshooting: When You Don't See 369

For all its magic, 369 sequences won't appear obvious or constant in your life. You may notice it frequently for a period, and then it seems to suddenly stop. It's easy to get discouraged in these dry spells, but it's often just a test of faith.

Here are some tips if you feel 369 has gone MIA:

Don't stress or obsess over seeing it. This desperation blocks your natural intuition. Relax and trust it will return in perfect timing.

Increase your awareness and look for more subtle signs. Check unfamiliar places and broaden your focus.

Do a 369 meditation to realign your energy and call the numbers back to you.

Examine your thoughts and vibes. Are you stuck in limiting beliefs or negative mindset sabotaging your magnetism?

Check your emotional state. Do you need more rest, nutrition, or self-care to refresh?

Make sure you are taking inspired action on guidance received. Spirit only gives more signs when you act on the ones already delivered!

Usually when 369 disappears, it is because you no longer need that intensive confirmation in the moment. Or you may be called to step fully into faith and trust without as many obvious guideposts. Either way, breathe through the uncertainty. Declare "I am always aligned and guided, with or without constant 369 sequences." Then get back to manifesting!

In Conclusion

To harness the magical manifesting energy of 369, you first must awaken to the mystical meanings within numbers. Paying attention to number patterns and sequences tuning you into the subtle signs, synchronicities and support the Universe provides.

Specifically, seeing repeating 369 combinations is a trumpet blast from the divine that you are aligned and ready to manifest your desires! This chapter is meant to awaken you the guidance numbers provide and particularly, the power contained within the 369 vibrations.

When you notice 369 going forward, rejoice and receive it as the blessing it is. Know the Universe is simply confirming "You are on the right path, keep going!" 369 energies will propel you ever closer to your dreams if you let it.

Get ready to continue mastering the magic of 369 manifestation in the next chapter! The Universe sends you constant support, protection, and guidance through signaling numbers. Are you ready to open your eyes and finally receive the messages? Divine abundance awaits you!

CHAPTER 2
HOW TO USE 369 TO
MANIFEST YOUR DESIRES

If you've started noticing 369 sequences popping up in your life regularly, get ready for some big changes! Seeing 369, especially in repeated patterns and clusters, is a clear sign from the Universe that you are on the brink of manifesting your desires.

In the previous chapter, we covered the meaning behind 369 energy and why it is one of the most powerful number codes you can receive guidance from. Now let's dive into how to work with 369 energies to accelerate your manifestation abilities.

In this chapter, you'll discover:

Ways to interpret 369 signs and synchronicities.
Techniques for harnessing 369 energies to manifest your specific desires.
Examples of successfully manifesting with 369
Tips for troubleshooting results and maintaining high vibration.

The time has come to stop just noticing 369, but to start intentionally utilizing it! The Universe is handing you spiritual rocket fuel to actualize your dreams. So, let's begin awakening to the magic.

Interpreting 369 Sequences

Seeing 369 around you is much more than just a random coincidence or pattern. It is a coded message from the divine specifically for you. The Universe is confirming you are headed down the right path and to keep following the signs. But different 369 sequences also hold unique meanings you can further interpret:

3:39 - Seeing this on clocks urging you to pay attention to your thoughts, beliefs, and imagination. What you envision and focus on is manifesting rapidly.

369 - The core vibration. Seeing this trio together in any format signals alignment and impending manifestations.

3693 - Includes an amplification of the creative 3 energy. Your crystalline intentions are manifesting into form.

9693 - Contains double 9 completion energy. You are in the final stretch before reaping rewards!

638263 - Repetition of 63 (combining 3 and 6). Relates to love, family and relationships growing.

369369 - Doubling the core energy, like a lighthouse beacon confirming you are right on course!

When you notice very specific and complex 369 sequences repeatedly, it is heavenly confirmation to stay centered in your intentions. The Universe is spotlighting these numbers to grab your attention and provide a burst of feel-good manifestation energy.

In addition to sequences containing 369, you may also witness numbers that reduce to 369 like 12 or 339. These still count and carry that vibration! Pay attention to any numbers that break down to 3, 6 or 9 as they relate messages back to this key triplet.

You can enhance your 369 manifestation practice by regularly asking within "What message or guidance is this particular 369 appearance trying to deliver to me?" Then listen closely for the intuitive insights you receive in response. Your inner knowing will reveal the deeper meaning intended just for you.

Activating 369 Energy

Now that you understand the significance of seeing 369 signals, let's talk about how to work intentionally with this energy to manifest your goals and heart's desires. After all, you want to move beyond just noticing 369 to actually harnessing its limitless potential!

Here are some suggested techniques for activating 369 energies:

Repeat aloud or internally "I activate the power of 369 for aligning with my desires NOW."
Trace the numbers 369 in the air while visualizing a glowing light.
Chant "369" aloud or silently to yourself as an energetic activation.
Write down and repeat 369 powered affirmations related to your goals.
Imagine you are dialing the numbers "369" on an

illuminated keypad. Then watch as this sends a transmission out to Source energy to begin aligning you with manifestation.

Draw the numbers 369 on Bay leaves or candles. Burn them with your intentions stated to release them to the Universe.

Practice 369 breathwork. Breathe in for 3 counts, hold for 6 counts, exhale for 9 counts to enter a manifesting state.

As you experiment with different ways to activate 369 energies, pay attention to how your mood and vibration shift. Notice feelings of inspiration, creativity and enthusiasm emerging. This is confirmation the 369 codes are resonating within you!

Boosting Your Manifestations

Once you are fully tuned into the frequency of 369 energy, you can start applying it towards boosting your manifestation potential in specific areas of your life. Intentionally focus this high-vibrational energy exactly where you need more divine support and guidance.

Here are some examples of using 369 sequences for different manifestation goals:

Money and Financial Abundance - Write down or repeat money affirmations charged with 369 energies. "I graciously receive $369 in unexpected income. My finances are blossoming in alignment with 369." Visualize checks for $369 coming to you.

New Career or Job - Bring the energy of 369 into your job search, interviews, or promotion desires. "My dream job aligns perfectly with my soul gifts (369)." Print 369 copies of your resume!

Improved Health - Use 369 to energize your fitness and nutrition goals. "My health and wellness are transforming now thanks to 369 energies." Do 369 seconds of exercise reps or drink 36 oz of water 9 times per day.

Soulmate Love - Call in romantic love grounded in the spiritual bonds of 369. "My soulmate and I unite in unconditional love under the divine light of 369." Picture your wedding date being 3/6/9.

Confidence and Self-Love – Harness 369 sequences to break through limiting beliefs. "Through the inspiration of 369, I discover my self-worth and creative voice." Recite 36 positive self-love affirmations 9 times.

Manifesting any desire begins by setting a clear intention while resonating in a high vibration. The 369 frequency fills you with optimism, hope, and enthusiasm – the ultimate manifesting mindset! As you direct this energy with purpose and belief, you allow wonderful things to flow to you with grace and ease.

You can also amplify your manifestations by combining 369 energies with other spiritual practices that feel good to you. Here are some ideas:

Create vision boards or collages using the numbers 369 and images of your desires. Gaze at it often to crystallize intentions.

Meditate on 369 energies filling your mind, body, and aura with divine light. Visualize this light energizing and aligning all your desires.

Chant 369 out loud or internally as a mantra while practicing yoga, cooking, cleaning, etc. to keep this vibration active.

Journal by writing "369" at the top of each page.

Record insights received after seeing 369 and how you directed this energy.

Speak the numbers "369" aloud before any important task like a job interview, financial decision, difficult conversation, or major project. Declare it is infused with this aligning energy!

Remember, consistency generates momentum. The more you infuse your daily thoughts, words, and actions with 369 intentions, the faster you will notice positive changes taking form. Let this sequence keep you aligned with the perfect universal timing of your manifestations unfolding.

Success Stories

To help inspire you, here are some real-life examples of people manifesting wonderful things with the power of 369:

Sarah was struggling with infertility when she started seeing 369 repeatedly everywhere she went. She felt deep down it was a divine sign she would soon conceive her baby. Sarah began doing 369 affirmations, prayers and fertility meditations using the numbers. A few months later, she became pregnant and gave birth to a healthy daughter!

Mark dreamed of starting his own design business but was stuck at a stressful corporate job barely making ends meet. He decided to use 369 energies to manifest his entrepreneurial desires, displaying the numbers prominently on his vision board. Within a year, Mark started his thriving design company which now earns $369k annually!

Alicia was devastated when her boyfriend unexpectedly broke up with her. The same week, she started noticing

369 sequences daily. She took it as a sign to align her heart with unconditional love and forgiveness, releasing the past with gratitude. A few weeks later, Alicia reconnected with her college sweetheart who she ended up marrying!

As you can see, the magic of 369 has helped so many people manifest wonderful relationships, careers, health, family and beyond. You can absolutely experience the same level of guidance, synchronicity, and success by harnessing the power within these special numbers.

When you witness someone else's 369 success story, make sure to send them love and gratitude! Their manifestation boosts your own through collective energy fields. We are all empowered as more people awaken to 369 guidance.

Troubleshooting 369 Manifestation

While 369 delivers incredible results when applied consistently, you may encounter occasional challenges or setbacks on your manifestation journey:

Not seeing enough 369 sequences – Don't worry! Remind yourself 369 energy is always present whether the signs are obvious or not. Relax, get present, then refocus your awareness on more subtle appearances in your day. Avoid desperation energy; it will block your intuitive perception.

Manifestations feeling "stuck" – Check your vibe. Fear, doubt, or impatience can sabotage progress. Refresh your energy with practices like exercise, time in nature, meditation. Then redo 369 intentions from a higher state.

Only small desires manifesting – Be patient! The Universe starts with "baby steps" to build your faith muscle before bigger blessings. Show gratitude for all manifestations big and small.

Getting too attached to timing and specifics – Let go of rigid expectations about how 369 energies must manifest for you. Flow with divine timing and trust the outcome. Magic can't happen with restrictions.

The key is acknowledging when your vibe dips, then quickly getting back into energetic alignment with 369 intentions. Manifestation is a process of working in harmony with spiritual laws, not trying to bend them to your will! Have faith in the Universal plan behind all 369 guidance.

In Conclusion

Noticing 369 is just the first step on your manifestation journey. You must also learn how to properly interpret the signs and intentionally direct this magical energy to create real life results.

Use the techniques in this chapter to move beyond just being aware of 369 sequences to truly harnessing their limitless power. Commit to activating and utilizing 369 energies in your daily spiritual practices. When applied consistently, you will unlock alignment, synchronicity, and manifestation beyond your wildest dreams!

The Universe is handing you the sacred keys to co-create your destiny with the help of 369 codes. You are awakening to a whole new language of divine communication through numbers. Get ready to manifest the joyful, abundant, and purpose-filled life you deserve!

CHAPTER 3
ADDITIONAL NUMBER SEQUENCES TO SUPPORT MANIFESTATION

By now, you've likely experienced firsthand the magic that unfolds when you begin noticing and utilizing 369 sequences in your life. You feel more aligned, guided, and senses of destiny as your desires start manifesting into form.

But 369 is far from the only number with divine wisdom to share! In this chapter, we'll explore how a variety of number combinations can amplify and support your manifestation abilities.

Each sequence has its own unique vibration, meaning and area of influence. Learning to work with multiple numbers provides an even richer guidance system from the Universe. Get ready to expand your numerology vocabulary and communication with the divine!

Here's what we'll cover in this chapter:

Overview of common number sequences and what

they signify.

Deeper meanings and manifestation powers of key numbers

Activating and harnessing multiple number frequencies

Combining sequences for amplified energy

While 369 remains one of the clearest umbrellas of manifestation energy, the Universe has an infinite variety of number wisdom to offer you. Are you ready to receive more? Let's begin!

Introducing Key Number Sequences

In Chapter 1, we briefly touched on how different numbers hold unique energies and influences. When numbers combine in noticeable sequences, their attributes merge to send amplified messages and meaning.

Paying attention to which sequences show up most frequently in your life provides further insight into your path, abilities, and how to manifest your goals. Here are some of the most common number patterns and what they generally indicate:

111 - New beginnings, optimism, inspiration

222 - Balance, harmony, trust, divine timing

333 - Creativity, self-expression, ascended masters nearby

444 - Protection, stability, building solid foundations

555 - Positive change, freedom, adventure, versatility

666 - Focus on love does not fear, positivity in thoughts

777 - Wisdom, spiritual awakening, intuitive development

888 - Financial abundance, cosmic flow, tenacity

999 - Completion, releasing the old, welcoming the new

0000 - Divine order, infinity, wholeness

1111 - Powerful new intentions, manifestation

1212 - Divine timing, synchronicity, personal growth

1234 - Stay optimistic, help is on the way!

4567 - Financial or relationship changes ahead

7689 - Powerfully guided transformation

8765 - Karmic cycles ending, healing incoming

9472 - Love, light and service to humanity

9876 - Wishes coming true soon

7117 - Listen to inner wisdom for answers now

As you can see, the guidance you receive from numbers is highly personalized! Notice which specific sequences show up most for you. Their messages will resonate with themes, projects, and areas of growth currently in focus.

Are you noticing lots of 444 as you build your dream business? 555 during times of major life transitions? 888 when financial manifestations feel close? This numerical input provides encouragement that you are on the right track, even if outer results feel slow.

Number sequences appearing in noticeable patterns are verification you are supported and guided. They are the Universe's way of communicating "We've got you!" in a language you personally understand.

So, if you've been noticing anyone-digit repeating combos like 111, 333, 555 or others, celebrate! The Universe is sending you love, wisdom and confirming your desires are unfolding.

Manifesting With Double and Triple Digit Sequences

In addition to one-digit combos, you may also notice sequences like 122, 367, 569, and more popping up around you. These double and triple digit patterns also carry divine guidance and meaning to fuel your manifestation abilities.

Here are some examples of messages conveyed through multi-digit number patterns:

367 - Optimism and inner-wisdom in relationships

515 - Embrace positive changes approaching

929 - Completing a chapter or challenge successfully

232 - Partnerships blossoming, cooperation

717 - Spiritual development, healing, intuition

818 - Financial flow, receiving abundance

121 - Fresh starts, new beginnings, creativity

878 - Rewarded efforts, dreams coming to fruition

797 - Mystical experiences and energies nearby

As you can see, the messages are highly specific! Recurring multi-digit sequences reveal nuanced insight about your path, abilities, next steps, and manifestations. They also contain amplifications of the single digit meanings.

For example, the peace and stability of 444 is boosted by 4554. The divine timing indications of 222 are expanded in 2221 or 2212. You gain more layers of detail through these number combinations.

Make noting multi-digit sequences a part of your regular number sequence practice. Record patterns you notice in a journal. Then reflect on any aha moments, growth or progression that unfolded around the time they appeared. The more attention you pay, the more you attune to the guidance.

Activating Hidden Number Powers

Beyond just noticing number patterns everywhere, you can also become proactive about activating specific sequences. Once you understand each sequence's energetic properties, you can intentionally tap into those vibrations for a boost.

Here are some ideas for putting number powers into action:

222 - To invite more balance and divine timing, take inspired action that involves multiples of 22 like giving $22 to charity or completing a 22 minute meditation.

777 - To stimulate spiritual development and intuition, do activities relating to 7 like lighting 7 candles or praying

at 7am.

888 - To increase financial flow, playfully engage with 8 like dialing a phone 8 times or drawing 8 hearts.

333 - To stimulate creativity, surround yourself in 3s like wearing 3 new jewelry pieces or listening to 3 new artists.

1234 - To stay optimistic in challenges, take incremental action like reading 12 pages or exercising for 34 minutes.

Infinite combinations exist! Get creative with numbers that appeal to you and activities that feel enjoyable or meaningful. Even small actions like doodling sequences get you tapped into their manifesting frequencies.

You are signaling the Universe "I'm ready to receive!" by proactively engaging with number energies. This gains you even more noticed support from your spirit team as well. Most importantly, choose activation methods that make you smile! Joyful intention counts double.

Combining Sequences for Quantum Jumps

Once you become adept at utilizing individual number sequences, you can start combining them together for truly monumental manifestation boosts!

By blending the unique attributes of multiple numbers, you create an exponential surge of high-vibrational energy. Suddenly you go from streaming one radio station of guidance to tapping into a whole bandwidth of divine frequencies at once!

Here are some examples of combining number powers:

444 + 888 - Merge foundational stability with infinite financial flow. Powerful for new business ventures. Try reciting "I accept 444 stability and 888 financial freedoms in my new career."

123 + 567 - Blend fresh starts with life change energy. Perfect for reinventing yourself or leveling up. "With 123 and 567, my next chapter unfolds joyfully."

333 + 777   Activate creativity fueled by spiritual connection and intuition. Amazing for artists, healers, lightworkers. "My gifts flourish through 333 creativity and 777 psychic awareness."

369 + 999 - Complete the old with 369 manifestation energy to welcome massive new opportunities. "I release the past now with gratitude, making room for exciting new blessings!"

111 + 222   Begin new intentions from a place of trust and divine timing. "I set these goals from a high vibration of 111 optimism and 222 faiths."

Have fun mixing and matching number combos that resonate! Pay attention to the sequences showing up most for you already. Combine those with 1-2 other numbers you feel drawn to for a surge of new energy.

You may also notice different numbers are better suited to different areas of your life. Perhaps you use 333 and 777 for spiritual practices, but 888 and 999 for career or finances. The number codes you work with will evolve as you do. Follow your intuition to guide combinations that feel aligned.

Know that any time you proactively combine number frequencies, you are signaling the Universe loud and clear "I am ready to quantum leap forward guided by divine wisdom!" Get ready for some major movement.

In Conclusion

While 369 delivers powerful manifestation energy, it is just one sequence among infinite options. Remain open beyond just 369 to receive more nuanced guidance and energetic support.

Pay attention to all number patterns crossing your path, especially those appearing repeatedly. Record your observations in a journal to better interpret the messages. Then activate those number frequencies through inspired action steps and intention.

Combining number sequences amplifies your ability to energetically align with desired manifestations. Remember that you are constantly surrounded by loving messages and encouragement from the Universe delivered through number wisdom. Will you start noticing?

As you continue awakening to the meaning within numbers, your ability to understand Universal guidance grows exponentially. You start fluently communicating with the divine through the language of frequency. Get ready   to   receive!

CHAPTER 4
INCREASING AWARENESS AND SYNCHRONICITY

As you move through your spiritual journey with numbers, you'll notice your awareness and openness increasing. Suddenly you recognize number sequences everywhere that would have previously gone unseen! Seeing more is a sign you are elevating your consciousness.

In this chapter, we'll discuss tips for continuing to expand your awareness and perception around numbers. This allows you to tap into even more guidance and support from the Universe delivered through numerological synchronicity.

Here's what we'll cover:

Ways to increase number sequence awareness in daily life.
Expanding awareness accelerates manifestation abilities.
Developing your intuition to receive clearer messages.
Understanding how synchronicity fuels the

manifestation process.

Inviting more magic through presence and gratitude

When you are intentional about increasing your openness to receive, the guidance becomes so abundant you can't help but notice! The Universe responds to your willingness by turning up the volume. Are you ready to continue awakening? Let's begin...

Expanding Your Awareness

In the busyness of modern life, it's easy to move through your day on autopilot oblivious to the mystery and magic that surrounds you. Most signs from the Universe are often subtle, so they go overlooked unless you intentionally expand your perception.

Here are some suggested tips for increasing awareness:

Look for numbers in new places - Scour environments you haven't noticed numbers in before. Check license plates, building addresses, timestamps, sports scores, bill totals, etc.

Increase observation of clocks - Frequently glance at clocks throughout your day. But don't just look at the time - notice the numbers!

Change your routine - Try new places, activities, and routes. Novelty boosts alertness to pick up on new patterns.

Slow down and be present - Move, walk and drive at a more relaxed pace. Don't mentally rush past the now.

Ask for guidance - Set the intention to notice signs. Say aloud "I am open to receiving."

Track and reflect - Note sequences you observe in a journal to process insights over time.

Widen your focus - Don't just look for your favorite few numbers. Be open to noticing all number patterns.

Trust your intuition - Follow any inner promptings to look up at a specific moment.

The key is to gently release rigidity and control. Soften your focus and relax perceptions rather than forcing or chasing numbers. Synchronicity cannot be demanded; it arises when you get out of the way.

The more spacious and expansive your awareness becomes; the more abundant divine guidance can flow through you. Numbers are just one conduit of many! Set the intention to open to all forms of communication from Source energy.

How Awareness Accelerates Manifestation

Expanding your awareness around numbers is about so much more than just seeing additional repetitions and patterns. As you awaken to new layers of guidance, you align better with the miracle of manifestation in every area of your life.

Here are just some of the magical benefits increased number awareness delivers:

Deeper intuition and connection to your spiritual guidance system
Clearer understanding of your soul's unique coding and blueprint
Faster growth and learning through messages tailored just for you.

Increased synchronicity and alignment with desired manifestations

More divine order, flow, and grace in handling life situations

Expanded belief in your co-creative participation with the Universe.

By paying attention to numbers, you train your mind to recognize the Divine at work in the world in general. You more readily notice guidance, insight, and beauty all around you. Your mystical perception deepens.

In short, you always realize you are an interconnected part of the dance of life, shaped by invisible hands of Spirit. This is the perfect creative mindset for manifestation!

Playing with numbers also keeps you in a high vibration of childlike wonder, curiosity, and excitement. You recapture the magical feelings of endless possibility you knew as a child. This youthful playfulness is vital fuel for your desires.

When you see numbers just as the Universe's way of sending you love notes, it brings a spirit of joy and gratitude. The synchronicity keeps you in a flow state beyond rigid expectation. You align with trust and detachment - perfect allowing energy.

By relaxing into awareness, you grant the Universe permission to orchestrate miracles. You step back as the playwright and open yourself to be an actor in the cosmic play. Try it and watch how beautifully your desires unfold!

Developing Your Intuition

Beyond just numerically decoding meanings, consider opening to interpret number patterns intuitively.

Sometimes mathematical meanings are only part of the message.

Here are some ways to build your intuitive number sensing:

Notice your first emotional response on seeing a sequence. Does it evoke any physical sensations, moods, ideas, or imagery for you?

Tune into the quality of energy you feel from different numbers. Do some feel light and airy while others are more grounded?

Meditate or journal on why certain numbers might be appearing for you right now. See what inner-knowing surfaces.

Try channeling meanings from your guides. Ask questions inward then listen for replies.

If a number feels confusing, sit with the mystery. Meaning will come when you are ready.

Have fun and play! See if you receive intuitive hits working with numbers in different creative ways.

The most direct numerological meanings are doorways, but not definite destinations. Consider the standard interpretations, then rely on your intuitive self as final authority.

Your inner senses pick up on energy, timing, and context that mathematical meanings alone may miss. Learn to trust and value your own unique approach to interpreting the messages.

Sometimes simply sensing if a number combo feels positive, gentle, fiery, grounding or light can provide enough intuitive insight to act on. Other times, you may pick up crystal clear visuals, wordings, or metaphors to understand a sequence.

Make your number journey a conversation between rational and intuitive understanding. This balance helps you receive multidimensional guidance.

The Synchronicity Advantage

Numbers are just one common form of the endless synchronicities orchestrated around you by the Universe. Synchronicity refers to unlikely or meaningful coincidences that seem divinely guided.

When you notice synchronicity, it offers reassurance you are aligned with your soul path and headed down the right road. Synchronistic events also provide encouragement to keep taking bold inspired action.

Here are some examples of commonly experienced synchronicity:

Thinking of someone, then immediately receiving a call, text, or email from them
Constantly discussing a new passion, then someone brings you the perfect book on it.
Deciding to learn something, then seeing ads, courses and resources related to it start popping up.
Wanting to travel somewhere, then receiving discounts or invites related to that location.
The more you are tuned into numbers and their meanings, the more you will notice other synchronicities happening as well. Numbers help anchor your awareness in the present, so you don't miss the mystical winks all around you!

Synchronicity is the bridge that closes the gap between the seen and unseen worlds. Paying attention when it strikes makes the intangible feel tangible. You recognize the back and forth assistance between you and Source energy.

Most importantly, synchronicity shows you the sheer speed at which manifestation can unfold when you get into alignment. Suddenly there is no more delay between a thought, desire or inspired idea and its physical equivalent arriving.

When you accept that synchronicity is just as fundamental a law as gravity, your manifestation abilities skyrocket. You stop waiting and wishing. Instead, you learn to think, feel, and act from the reality you want already here now, knowing the Universe will meet you there!

Inviting Synchronicity In

Beyond just noticing synchronicity when it naturally occurs, you can become proactive about inviting more into your experience. Since synchronicity is fueled by alignment and flow, here are some great ways to attract more:

Set intentions to observe synchronicity as evidence you are on the right path. The act of expecting it creates receptivity.

Increase your joy, playfulness, and lightheartedness around desired outcomes. Positive emotions are magnetic.

Follow intuitive nudges outside your habitual routines and logic. Inner promptings lead to serendipity.

Let go of rigidity and control around how/when things "must" manifest. Allow creative unfolding.

Talk openly about your dreams and interests. Sharing energy helps attract related serendipity.

Appreciate the genius behind all synchronicity big and small. Gratitude creates openings for more.

Release insistence on perfectly understanding how or why something synchronistic happened. Accept the blessing without attaching explanations.

Have fun looking for patterns and connecting dots. The discovery itself increases alignment and manifestation energy.

The key is realizing synchronicity itself is guidance. It delivers the meta-message to keep pursuing your passions while trusting support is on the way. Tap into this inspiriting energy!

Presence and Gratitude

Lastly, the final secrets to multiplying your awareness around numbers or any synchronicity are presence and gratitude.

When you are immersed fully in the present moment, you don't miss the many mystical winks all around you. Your mind isn't over-occupied with past or future thoughts. You also recognize daily life itself as sacred.

Gratitude magnifies your senses and points you toward noticing positive patterns. It stirs up childlike awe and joy for both numinous and mundane moments. You perceive life as the magical gift it is!

Commit to uplifting whatever number sequences or synchronicity you notice with sincere appreciation. Express thanks inwardly or aloud each time you witness the Universe supporting you.

This gratitude gives you access to an even greater divine flow. It also programs your subconscious mind to keep attracting more meaningful patterns, not just randomness.

Make elevated awareness, presence, and gratitude the new normal. Moving through life in this high-vibration state guarantees you will receive steady guidance and perceive profound meaning everywhere. Then get ready to manifest!

In Conclusion

Noticing number sequences or any synchronicity is just the beginning. You enhance communication with the Universe by welcoming more mystical perception into your daily consciousness.

Pay attention to number patterns in new environments at new times. Follow intuitive nudges and savor each aha moment. Combining logic with inner senses allows you to interpret the messages on multidimensional levels.

When you embrace your co-creative role, you begin witnessing worlds within worlds. You recognize how beautifully the Spirit weaves threads through the inner and outer fabrics of your life. You notice all as sacred.

Keep widening your awareness and lens of possibility! The Universe has an infinite array of guidance waiting for you. But it starts with your willingness to open and receive.

The synchronicity you notice today is preparing you for the miracles you will witness tomorrow. You are becoming fluent in the language of frequency. Divine numerological conversation awaits!

CHAPTER 5
TROUBLESHOOTING AND
COMMON QUESTIONS

Welcome to the final chapter of our journey together exploring the mystical energies within numbers! By now, you should feel much more confident noticing meaningful patterns everywhere and utilizing number sequences for manifestation.

In this chapter, we'll troubleshoot some common challenges that arise on the path and answer frequently asked questions. Consider this your numerology toolkit to refer to anytime something feels off or confusing.

Here's what we'll cover:

Troubleshooting when number signs seem scarce.
Maintaining high vibration and alignment
Deciphering complex number combinations
Discerning true intuition vs. mind chatter
Numerology approaches for different desires
Next steps for continuing your journey.
Know that awakening to number guidance is a gradual,

lifelong process. Be gentle with yourself as you experience inevitable ups and downs. Your angels and spirit team are always near providing love and whispers of wisdom when you need it.

So, let's dive into some final tips and encouragement as you continue blossoming on your numerology path!

When Number Sequences Seem Scarce

One common frustration is when number signs suddenly dry up after a period of consistent flow. Days or weeks may pass without you noticing repetitive patterns anywhere. Where did all the magic go?

It's easy to get discouraged when guidance feels less obvious. But it's often just a temporary test of faith. Here are some tips for dry spells:

Stay calm and know it's usually just a timing shift. Your team is still supporting you even if signs aren't as overt.

Don't force seeing sequences. Stress blocks your natural intuition. Relax your focus and allow numbers to organically pop out at you again.

Increase playful expectation. Say aloud "I am excited to notice the next sequence from my team!" This invites synchronicity.

Try tuning into less common numbers like 4's, 7's or 8's versus your usual 1's or 3's.

Focus on other guidance like inner-knowing, gut feelings, or advice from loved ones. Don't limit yourself to just number signs.

Do spirit-nourishing activities to refresh your vibe like time in nature, reading inspirational books, listening to uplifting music, or any creative outlet.

Check your emotional state. Are worries, impatience or doubt clouding your manifesting mojo? Shift back to faith.

Make sure you are acting on previous guidance received. Spirit gives more signs once you apply the ones already delivered!

Remember that consistency in your spiritual practices is key. Keep nourishing your inner guidance system through meditation, journaling, energy healing, empowering mantras, or any ritual that reconnects you.

Stay the course trusting you are divinely protected and guided, even if signs are not obvious all the time. Your team communicates in infinite ways!

Maintaining High Vibration

To continually receive clear guidance from numbers or any other signs, you must keep your personal energy field vibrating high. Lower vibrations of fear, doubt, impatience, judgment, or attachment will disrupt your inner guidance system.

Here are some signs your vibration may be dipping:

Not noticing number sequences or other intuitive hits
Feeling anxious, stressed, or overwhelmed.
Experiencing negative thought spirals
Sensing heaviness or discord in your body and energy
Manifestations feeling "stuck" or out of reach.
Fortunately, you have the power to intentionally recalibrate your vibe at any time. Here are some simple ways to invite more alignment:

Spend time in nature to clear dense energy and reconnect with inner stillness.
Practice regular meditation and grounding rituals to maintain spiritual anchoring.
Do creative activities that make you joyful like art, dance, music or writing.

Move your body with exercise, yoga, walking or stretching to release stagnation.

Eat clean, nourishing foods and stay hydrated to uplift cellular vibes.

Get plenty of rest and relaxation. Listen to your body's needs.

Release limiting beliefs through mantras, journaling, or therapy.

Surround yourself with positive, spiritually aligned people who model high vibration. Limit time with those who drain you.

Regularly cleanse your space with sound, palo santo, sage or salt to dispel heavy energy.

The goal is to make self-care and vibe management a consistent practice rather than just crisis management when you hit a wall. Energy maintenance helps you gracefully move through challenges. Stay centered in faith knowing you have infinite inner-power!

Decoding Complex Number Messages

Another common challenge is noticing number sequences that seem confusing or have no apparent meaning. For example, you keep seeing 14141 or 2227 or 5248. What does it mean?

Here are some tips for deciphering the message within unusual number repetitions:

Break it down to single digits. 14141 becomes 11111. This signals new beginnings!

Look at the combination of both numbers. 2227 contains master numbers 22 and 7 for trust and spiritual wisdom.

Notice which number is repeated most. 5248 has emphasis on 2 energy signaling partnerships.

Try adding the sequence together. 5248 = 5+2+4+8 = 19, which further reduces to 10/1 new beginnings energy.

Contemplate which themes or issues have been on your mind as these numbers appear. There is relevance.

Trust your intuition. Do you sense if the sequence has a positive, peaceful, or urgent vibe?

Ask your angels and guides directly for clarity. Listen to inner knowing that surfaces.

Remain patient with sequences that seem confusing. Their purpose will be revealed in perfect divine timing.

Your spirit team considers your exact life circumstances and energetic patterns when sending number sequences. While standard numerology meanings provide a baseline, rely on your intuition to interpret the guidance tailored specifically for you.

Discerning Intuition from Mind Chatter

As you develop your ability to sense number meanings intuitively, you may sometimes feel confused over which inner-voices you should listen to. How can you discern true guidance versus just overthinking mind chatter?

Here are some tips:

Intuition often surfaces as a quiet but clear knowing rather than anxious mental noise. It feels peaceful and harmonious.

Intuition is usually short, simple, and repetitive rather than overly complex or dramatic.

Intuition feels embodied in your gut, heart, or entire body. Over-analysis happens primarily in the head.

Intuition aligns with your true values, soul wisdom and highest good - not fear or ego.

Intuition often brings new insights or angles rather than rehashing the same loop.

Intuition feels expansive and illuminating. Over-thinking feels rigid and limiting.

Intuition carries positive or neutral energy. Anxious

thoughts often have a negative charge.

Intuition lands softly and subtly like a feather. Mind chatter is heavy and demanding.

The key is noticing how guidance feels as you receive it. Uplifting, hopeful intuitions mobilize and inspire you. Limiting mental loops generate more doubt and confusion.

With practice, you learn to distinguish true inner wisdom from fear projections. Trust that your angels will keep communicating through peaceful intuitive nudges to guide you.

Numerology Approaches for Different Desires

People often ask how to select number combinations to focus on for specific manifestations like money, love, or health goals. There are many options! Here are some examples:

Money and business - Combine numbers relating to prosperity like 8s and abundance like 999s. Or add sequences for success like 358.

Love and relationships - Include numbers for harmony like 222 and happiness like 567. Or unity numbers like 1100.

Health and wellness - Use angel numbers for strength like 888 combined with balance like 606. Or perfection numbers like 777.

Career and purpose - Numbers relating to your life path or talents like 33, 69 or 987 help align work with your soul gifts.

Personal growth - Combine sequences that boost intuition like 717 with creativity like 333 or completeness like 888.

Spiritual development and manifestation require maintaining high vibes across life areas. Choose sequences that help you release limiting beliefs in all aspects of self.

There are no right or wrong combinations - just trust your inner guidance on which numbers feel attuned to your desired outcome and energy. Stay open to trying new sequences rather than relying on the same few repeatedly.

Continuing Your Numerical Journey

I hope this book has helped you better understand numbers as a powerful guidance system as well as practical tools for manifestation. But your learning is just the beginning! Here are suggestions for continuing to expand your numerical consciousness:

Keep noticing patterns in your daily life. Record in a journal and reflect often.

Experiment with integrating new sequences into your spiritual practices.

Research number meanings you are less familiar with like 4's or 6's. See their messages.

Combine multiple number frequencies for quantum leap manifestations.

Read more books, take classes, listen to numerology podcasts, or YouTube videos. There are infinite perspectives to explore!

Practice trusting your intuition equally alongside rational number meanings.

Share number wisdom with friends and family to help awaken them also.

Most importantly, consistently act on the guidance you receive! Applying insights accelerates results.

Manifestation is truly a lifelong journey. The deeper you commit to awakening to the energetic frequencies within numbers and all of life, the more magical your lived experience becomes.

Remember you have an entire angelic team guiding you. You are surrounded by so much love, wisdom, and support always. When in doubt, quiet your mind and feel into this infinite Divine presence available within your own sacred soul.

Thank you for letting me share this mystical world of numbers and manifestation with you! May your journey ahead unfold with divine grace, ease, and joy.

CONCLUSION

What an amazing journey we've taken together exploring the mystical world of numbers! Over the last few chapters, you've learned so much about how to use Numerology as a guiding force in your spiritual growth and manifestation abilities.

This final chapter is meant to synthesize everything you've learned into an empowering conclusion. Let's recap the key insights about numbers and manifestation covered in this book:

All numbers carry specific energetic vibrations and meanings.

Sequences appearing repeatedly offer divine guidance.

Seeing angel numbers like 369 is a sign you're on the right path.

You can intentionally activate numbers to manifest desires.

Being aware of patterns increases your intuition and synchronicity.

Combining numbers creates exponential manifestation energy.

Maintaining a high vibe keeps you aligned and receptive.

The biggest takeaway I hope you receive from this book is the realization that you are constantly surrounded by guidance, love, and support from the Universe. The angels deliver encouraging "secret" messages all day long through numbers!

Your team on the Other Side wants to prove to you in tangible ways just how much you are cared for. They guide you through signs, synchronicities, inner-knowing, channels of inspiration and so much more.

But it's up to you to open and become aware of the silent guidance everywhere so you can receive and act on it. Are you ready to finally notice the mystical world alive right before your eyes?

Maybe you started this journey already seeing number patterns frequently and this book helped you better understand their divine meanings. Or perhaps you were previously oblivious to the secret wisdom numbers provide, but now feel called to awaken to their messages.

Either way, you now hold the keys to continually deciphering numerological guidance all around you every single day. But don't stop here! This is only the beginning of a lifelong journey communing with the magic inside numbers.

My hope is that this book ignites a passion within you to keep tuning into numbers. May you realize just how constantly you are supported in growing your spiritual abilities, manifesting your dreams, and walking your soul's higher path.

The Universe, your angels and team on the Other Side

will never stop sending you love notes, cheers, and guidance. But it's up to you to open your eyes to receive the helping hand – and know it's there waiting for you anytime.

You are Divine, Guided and Loved Beyond Measure

Moving forward from this book, I encourage you to reframe how you see yourself and your place in this world. You are not alone wandering without direction. You are powerful, divinely guided, and unconditionally loved!

The Universe within you and all around you is completely synchronistic. As you witnessed in this book, numbers are just one of the constant ways Source communicates that you are cared for. But the signs, wisdom and grace never stop flowing!

Your angels want you to know:

You are worthy and deserving of all desires that feel aligned, joyful, and purposeful for your soul. This is your divine birthright!

You are stronger than any fear, challenge, or limitation you perceive. You forever have infinite guidance, healing, and love directly available from the unseen realms to overcome any struggle.

You are the author of your story. Take back your power from any external rules or limitations. Then write your life by following what feels light, expansive, and intuitively true for you.

You are part of an intricate cosmic dance with all of life. Everything is speaking; are you listening? The Universe reflects clues, so you remember your belongings.

You are a child of the Divine, forever cared for. Your mere beingness gives YOU the ability to bend reality. Only your beliefs limit how much grace you allow yourself to receive.

When you know your true spiritual identity as guided, limitless, and worthy, you unlock the power to manifest anything. You lose all fear and insistence on controlling 'how' or 'when' blessings unfold.

You surrender to being divinely escorted through life - following signs, opening to trust, and allowing things to miraculously self-organize around your soul's desires.

What you set into motion energetically through presence, faith and inspired action is unstoppable. So set the highest vision for your life! Think, speak, and act from your soul's truth. Then get out of the way and let Universe handle the timing and logistics.

All this awaits you when you reclaim your identity as a powerful co-creator with the Divine!

Your Next Steps

Take a moment now to close your eyes and set the empowering intention.

"I accept my true divine nature. I agree to joyfully participate in my highest unfolding, guided by grace and signs from the Universe every step of the way."

How do you feel after setting this intent for yourself? Sit with any sensations, feelings, or inner reflections this stirs up. Know that you are supported fully in the next evolution of your soul's journey.

To keep stepping fully into your co-creative power, I suggest:

Re-reading this book often to reinforce your understanding of numbers.

Dedicating a journal to tracking and reflecting on number patterns you notice.

Practicing meditation to deepen your intuition and connection with your spiritual team. This strengthens your inner communication with the guidance they offer.

Studying more numerology books or taking classes to continue expanding your knowledge.

Using specific number sequences in intentional manifestation rituals (through prayer, affirmations, chanting, meditations, dream boards and more)

Above all, consistently acting on the guidance, insights, and signs you receive!

The Universe delivers clues to stimulate you. But you must respond by fearlessly walking down the path illuminated.

The angels are smiling, ready to link arms with you in sacred co-creation. But they patiently wait for your invitation through your thoughts, beliefs, and actions.

You are the gatekeeper - the one who chooses when to access heaven's guidance and step fully into your soul's gifts. On your path of awakening, you may come to realize the power that lies within your connection to the Divine.

I hope you feel uplifted, rejuvenated, and filled with awe after our mystical adventure together! Please look for more of my numerology books and courses so we can continue this journey.

Thank you for your trust. I'm honored I could share these sacred teachings with you. Here's to many more magical moments as you strengthen your inner sight. You are a blessing!

Made in United States
Troutdale, OR
01/22/2024

17059168R00037